SHELLEY ROTNER

GROW!
RAISE!
CATCH!

HOW WE GET OUR FOOD

HOLIDAY HOUSE / NEW YORK

A long time ago there were no stores or refrigerators. To survive, people had to grow, gather, hunt and fish for their food.

Milk came right from the cow every morning. Eggs were gathered from the chickens. Butter and cheese were made at home. People ate vegetables, fruits, meat and fish as soon as they were harvested or caught, or they *preserved* them to eat after the growing season was over.

EGGS FROM OUR ORGANICALLY FED PASTURE RAISED HAPPY HENS $6 DOZ

Today most people buy their food from stores. However, more people are buying fresh foods locally at farmer's markets or farm stands.

But where does the food come from, and whom can we thank for producing it?

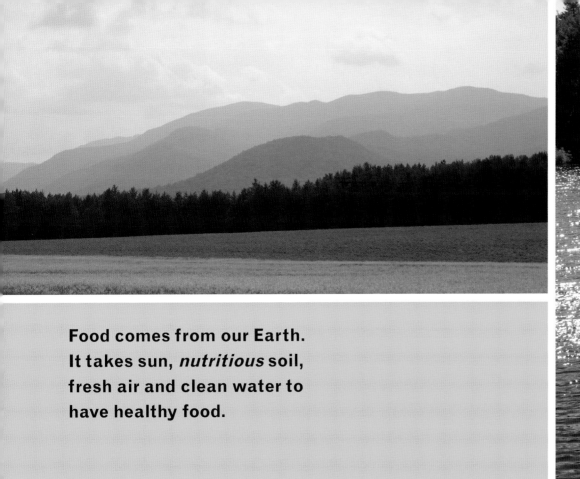

Food comes from our Earth.
It takes sun, *nutritious* soil,
fresh air and clean water to
have healthy food.

We can thank
our farmers
and fishermen
for our food.
They grow the
vegetables,
grains and
fruits, they
raise the
animals and
catch the fish
that we eat.

"I'm a **VEGETABLE FARMER.** I love to plant seeds in my fields and see the greens grow and grow. When they're ripe and ready, I *harvest* them so you can have fresh, delicious salad too!"

Lettuce is a leaf vegetable. Even though it's mostly made up of water, it's very nutritious.

Tomatoes are usually red, but they can be green, purple, yellow, white, black, pink, orange or even striped.

Peppers can taste sweet or spicy hot.

Carrots grow underground.

Cucumbers grow on creeping vines.

"We're VEGETABLE FARMERS. We love to grow peppers, carrots, cucumbers and tomatoes."

"We're **BERRY FARMERS.** We grow mostly blueberries on bushes on our farm because they taste good, they're good for you and they grow well in the soil where we live."

Blueberries are one of the only natural foods that are blue.

Strawberries are the only fruit that has seeds on the outside, not on the inside. They are the first fruit to ripen every spring.

Raspberries are usually red, but they can be black, purple and yellow too. The plant has sharp thorns.

Buy Local
Dutton's
BLUEBERRIES
$3 95
PINT

"I'm a *CITRUS* FARMER. I grow orange trees in groves where the weather stays warm all year round."

Most oranges are made into juice.

"We're **FRUIT FARMERS.**
We grow peaches and
crispy apples on trees in
an *orchard*. We like to see
them grow from buds
to flowers to delicious
ripe fruit."

**It takes about
thirty-six apples
to make a gallon
of cider. There are
over 700 kinds of
peaches.**

100% ALL NATURAL
PREMIUM
APPLE CIDER

MADE FROM A SELECT BLEND OF FRESH, RIPE APPLES
PASTEURIZED TO ENSURE FRESHNESS
INGREDIENTS: Freshly Squeezed Apple Cider
No Water, No Sugar, No Concentrate, No Preservative Added
REFRIGERATE BELOW 42° SHAKE WELL
1/2 GAL (1.89L)   Dep.
                                     ME 5¢

"I'm a **WHEAT FARMER.** Wheat is a kind of grass that has been growing for a very long time. I love to see the golden fields of wheat swaying in the wind."

Wheat grains are ground up to make flour. Bread, spaghetti, tortillas and cereal are often made with wheat flour.

"I'm a **RICE FARMER.**
I grow rice in wet fields
called paddies. Rice is
the seed of a certain
kind of grass."

**Rice feeds half
the world's
population. There
are 40,000 kinds
of rice, but brown
rice is the most
nutritious.**

"We're **POTATO FARMERS.**
It's been in our blood for
seven generations. The
plants have white flowers.
It's beautiful to see the
fields in bloom. We like to
harvest and dig them up
because it's always a bit of
a surprise."

**Potatoes come in
many different colors,
shapes and sizes.**

"I'm a **CORN FARMER**. I grow corn on stalks in fields. The leafy part of the plant grows ears, which contain the seeds, called kernels."

Popping the kernels of a certain kind of corn makes popcorn. Corn always has an even number of rows.

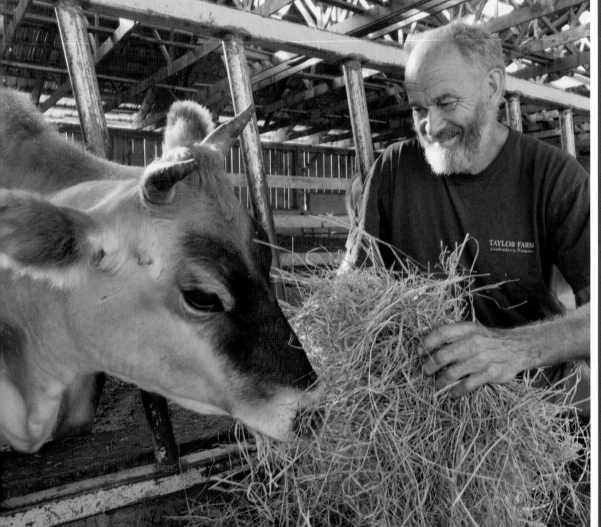

"I'm a **DAIRY FARMER. I** raise cows for their milk. They're curious animals and creatures of habit. They always come into the barn in the same order."

Milk is the main ingredient in butter, cheese, yogurt and ice cream. Yum!

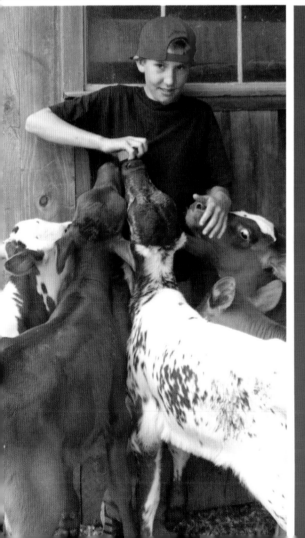

"I'm a BEEF FARMER. I raise cattle for their meat. I love seeing the cows out in the pasture."

Cows eat mostly grass. Hamburgers and steak come from cattle.

"I'm a **CHICKEN FARMER.** I like to listen to the many sounds they make to say they're happy or to sound a warning against a *predator*. It takes a chicken a whole day to lay an egg, and after they do, they cluck."

Eggs come in different colors depending on the chicken's breed.

"I'm a **PIG FARMER.** I raise pigs for their meat. They're really smart animals."

Pork comes from pigs: pork chops, bacon, hot dogs and pepperoni are all made from pork.

Little Ne
Cherrystc
Quahaugs
Oysters..
Mussels..

"I'm a FISHERMAN. I catch big ocean fish. I like to be on a boat far from land, although deep-sea fishing is hard work."

Fish often swim together in groups called schools.

"I'm a SHELLFISH FARMER. I dig for clams and harvest scallops and oysters."

These fish have hard shells for protection.

"I'm a **LOBSTER FISHERMAN.** I catch lobsters with traps out in the ocean."

Lobsters shed their shells as they grow.

"We have a **FAMILY FARM**. We raise chickens for eggs and meat and goats for milk. We also grow our own vegetables and fruits. We raise bees and get honey from the hives. We tap the sap from our maple trees to make maple syrup. We make jelly from our grapes. We get sunflower seeds from our sunflowers. We like to know where our food comes from. We *compost* our leftover scraps of food by putting them back into the soil to make the soil healthier and more fertile. Then our food and animals will be healthier too."

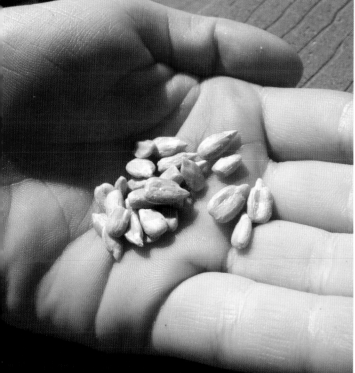

People can **GROW** their own food in gardens or pots in the country or city. Some cities have *community gardens* and rooftop gardens.

**Dedicated to the
farmers and fishermen
who work so hard to
bring us food**

—S.R.

Did You Know?

You are what you eat! Healthy foods free of chemicals
and pesticides picked at the peak of ripeness and eaten
fresh are delicious and good for you. They have *vitamins*,
minerals and nutrients that help your body grow and
stay strong. The most wholesome dairy and meat come
from healthy animals raised eating nutritious food and
drinking clean water. Fruits and vegetables like peppers,
tomatoes, oranges, strawberries and blueberries contain
vitamin C that helps keep you from getting sick.

Leafy greens, apples, peaches, cucumbers, carrots,
potatoes, eggs, fish and whole grains all have vitamins
that help keep your blood and nervous system strong
and fight off diseases.

Dairy products, such as milk and cheese, provide
minerals that build strong bones and teeth.

Meats, nuts, seeds, beans and whole grains have protein
and iron to help your body grow and stay healthy.

Glossary

Citrus: juicy fruits such as lemons, oranges or grapefruits
that have thick rinds and grow on trees or shrubs in warm
places.

Community garden: a piece of land gardened by a
cooperative group of people living in the neighborhood.

Compost: food wastes such as vegetable peels and
eggshells that are broken down or rotted. When mixed
back into the soil, compost enriches the soil. Composting
reduces the amount of garbage sent to landfills.

Growing season: the part of the year when fruits,
vegetables and other plants grow successfully.

Harvest: to gather food that is ready to be eaten.

Nutritious: having substances such as vitamins and
minerals that a person or animal needs to grow properly
and stay healthy.

Orchard: an area planted with fruit trees.

Predator: an animal that hunts for other animals.

Preserve: the process of treating food to last over time
either by freezing, canning, salting or drying.

Vitamins: nutrients that your body needs to
work properly. They help your body grow and stay
healthy and strong.

Copyright © 2016 by Shelley Rotner. All Rights Reserved.
HOLIDAY HOUSE is registered in the U.S. Patent and Trademark Office.
Printed and Bound in April 2017 at Toppan Leefung, DongGuan City, China.
www.holidayhouse.com   10 9 8 7 6 5 4 3 2
Designed by Hans Teensma, Impress
Library of Congress Cataloging-in-Publication Data
Names: Rotner, Shelley, author.   Title: Grow! Raise! Catch! : how we get our
food / by Shelley Rotner.   Description: New York : Holiday House, [2016]
Identifiers: LCCN 2015040849 | ISBN 9780823436439 (hardcover)
Subjects: LCSH: Food—Juvenile literature. | Farmers—Juvenile literature.
| Fishers—Juvenile literature. Classification: LCC TX355 .R672 2016 | DDC 641.3—dc23
LC record available at http://lccn.loc.gov/2015040849

ISBN 978-0-8234-3884-6 (paperback)